Dating

The Secret to Attracting the Woman of Your Dreams and Creating a Fulfilling Relationship

Thomas Angelo

Introduction

After diligently working on myself, at the age of 27, I had my first "official girlfriend." Mind you, growing up all through adolescence and early adulthood, I had many 'OK' relations with women and met many women I felt I had a chance with but it eventually failed to work out. I also had various relationships with women who, after being together for a short while, would no longer want anything to do with me.

I had a challenging childhood. Of the many things I struggled with as a young person, being in a fulfilling romantic relationship with a woman was always at the top of my list of areas of my life full of painful memories.

I grew up with very domineering parents and spent most of my young life with my mum and grandmother (women) so much so that I adopted many feminine qualities, something that revealed itself when I started dating.

I was a shy guy who lacked confidence. Further, my approach and ability to manage stressful situations were terrible. Each time I thought about walking up to a woman I liked and making my move, I would get extremely nervous and give up, or go for it only to end up making a fool of myself. The women I dated would later dump me because I was "too needy."

With several painful memories, rejections, and an inability to approach the women I felt genuinely attracted to, I felt miserable. My emotional turmoil was so grave that if my closet walls could talk, they would tell a tale of a man who has cried in the closest many times.

Unhappy with the results I was getting, and out of desperation and a strong desire to improve my dating and relationship life, I spent years studying any material I could find on dating and relationships. I spent many hours reading books and watching YouTube videos and online lectures.

These investments in books, lectures, and seminars helped me deal with the memories of my painful rejections, and gave me the motivation I needed to continue putting myself out there in spite of the failures and challenges I had to deal with during the dating and relationship learning process.

After taking **massive action** and **applying** the knowledge I distilled from various books, videos, and online lectures, my dating and relationship life, understanding, and knowledge of women improved, and my confidence is now better compared to how it was. I have now dated many women, many of whom I have felt attracted to, have had several successful relationships, and I am a happier and more confident man.

So, why did I write this book? I wrote this book out of a personal desire to help other men who are struggling with dating and relationships. The pain I experienced was terrible, and I know that many men are experiencing the same pain and going through similar situations.

My aim for writing this book is to help you become the best version of yourself by mastering dating and romantic relationships with women. My promise to you is that the money you used to purchase this book is a worthwhile investment in yourself, an investment that will repay itself tenfold.

This book will reveal to you ideas and strategies that when implemented, will help you master your dating and relationship life. I am confident that the material here will help you.

Is this Book For You?

I will now ask you some questions. How you choose to answers these questions will reveal whether this book is for you.

If you answer YES to a substantial percentage of these questions, this book is for you, and from it, you will learn invaluable strategies that'll help improve your dating and relationship life.

Have you ever had a crush on a woman but felt too 'afraid' to make a move?

Have you ever asked yourself why the women you want and find attractive never want you or why the women that are crazy about you are the ones you are not so "crazy" about?

Are you a nice guy, the kind of man that women tend to use?

Are you a nice guy that frequently gets friend zoned and women do not want any romantic relations with you?

Are you the guy who gets no respect from women?

Is approaching a woman you find attractive a challenge?

Was she initially interested in you, but for some reason, she no longer wants you and will not tell you why?

Did you recently experience a painful rejection and now feel as if your dating life is over?

Has your girlfriend or wife stopped loving you?

Have you met a beautiful woman, but when you ask her out on a date, she gives you excuses that don't explain why she doesn't want to go out on a date with you?

Have you ever asked a woman why she would not go out with you and never got a straight answer?

Have you ever felt that a woman liked you, and she even gave you her phone number, but then would never go out with you?

Have you ever had women cancel dates at the last minute for BS reasons?

Do you feel like women don't make sense at all?

Do you ignore dating and relationship altogether and focus on other aspects of your life, such as business and other hobbies?

Are you the guy that women say "you're such a gentleman" or "you're such a nice guy," but then she doesn't want to go out with you?

The first step to solving a problem is admitting the existence of the problem. Things started changing for me when I acknowledged the problem. By accepting that my dating and relationship life was not going as well as I would have hoped, my mindset changed to one focused on growth and learning. Today I focus on daily growth.

If you see yourself in any one of the points above, know that I know how you feel because I have been there. I also commend you for buying this book; it shows your commitment to self-growth and your readiness to embark on a self-transformative journey.

Table of Contents

Chapter 1: Become Your Best and Strongest Self

In addition to essential strategies whose application of will help you become better at attracting the woman of your dreams and having a fulfilling relationship, the knowledge you take from this book will help better other areas of your life. It will help you become your best self.

A friend once said to me, "Thomas, I don't understand why you're struggling with women. You have the looks, the money, good career, etc. I don't even have what you have, and I'm broke as well, but look at how great I am with women." He continued, "If I had what you have, my dating life would be crazy." My friend was right.

He was a pro with women, someone who could get any girl he wanted. Sometimes he would have multiple girls chasing him and falling for him, a guy who was seriously broke and just staying at home with his mum. I saw girls travel from other cities to see him. My friend just had an abundance of women and would sometimes introduce some of them to his friends.

My friend has had all kinds of beautiful women fall for him and being broke; he wasn't even spending that much. He would often say, *"Thomas, it's not always about the money,"* and he was right. He once told me about this beautiful woman he dated who would pay for date nights and do all kinds of things to get his attention. I learned a lot from him.

So, let us learn why most men struggle with dating.

1.1: Why Most Men Struggle With Women and What It Means To Be Your Best Self

Most men struggle with women because they are not being their best self, which is in itself because there is a limitation in their mind holding them back from experiencing life to the fullest. To start attracting the woman of your dreams into your life and courting her appropriately, you have to come from a place of strength.

What goes on in your mind when you see a beautiful woman from across the street? What happens to your mind, when you see a woman across the street that you would like to ask on a date? Do you freely walk up to her and strike up a conversation, or do you freeze in thoughts?

Many men have no problem with talking to women they are not attracted to; but as soon as they meet a gorgeous woman they genuinely like, they are no longer their natural self.

Most men see a beautiful woman as a superior being; they then put her up on a pedestal to a point where conversations become so awkward, and because of the invisible radar all women have, they drop such a guy quickly because he is weak and lacking confidence. Your first interaction with a woman is critical. If you fail at creating a good impression, getting her to see you as a potential romantic partner will be that much harder.

Most of my successful relationships with women are those where the first impression was great. In the courtships where I came off as weak and unconfident in our first interaction, no matter what I did later, the relationship didn't work out for me.

I usually advise men to walk away when they fail in the first, second, and third interactions. Doing this will save you a lot of time, pain, and energy. If you're struggling to attract the woman of your dreams, it's because you're not your best and strongest self.

But, how then do you become your best self?

1.2: What It Takes to Become Your Best, Strongest Self

The process of becoming your best and strongest self is a self-transformative journey that starts with embracing self-growth, which in this case, entails the following:

Become Whole

Women find neediness and desperation very unattractive. If you are needy and desperate, even if you date her, she will eventually dump you. You shouldn't need a woman to feel good about yourself. A purposeful man is an attractive man. Seek a whole, purpose-driven life!

Do things that bring you joy and fulfillment, and which give you a sense of completeness. Are you living a whole life? In the absence of somebody to say you look nice, do you feel great, as someone who is working towards personal betterment?

Do not put women on a pedestal; it will make you feel inferior when you are around beautiful women. Feeling inferior is a big turn off. Love and value yourself, and see yourself as attractive and deserving of the woman of your dreams.

Believe in Yourself and Cultivate Self-Confidence

I have had many male friends who seem "challenged in the looks department" but who are dating gorgeous women. What I noticed about these men is their sense of self-belief. Whenever I was in the company of one, even before approaching a woman, he would say, "Do you see that girl over there? I am going to ask her out and date her."

From this mentality, such a man is not thinking about "how or whether" it would work out with the girl, no; he is only thinking about "when" he attracts, courts, and gets the woman. Such men are an exception, not the rule.

Unfortunately, when most men see a beautiful woman, the first thought that comes to mind is the thought of "being turned down" or the woman being out of his league. Because of such a mindset, such a man eventually gets the exact result he thought of: the woman rejects him. Do you know why? Because by operating from an inferiority complex, the man is operating under the false impression that a beautiful woman would not want anything to do with him. Such a man sees himself failing long before approaching. Such a man cannot attract the woman of his dreams.

From this, it's easy to see how your mind or thought could be sabotaging you and affecting what you can experience with women? This area of your life is one that I strongly encourage you to work on because mastering it will help you with women and prove invaluable in other areas of your life.

Don't be a "Nice Guy."

I define a Nice Guy as a weak man who doesn't have any self-respect and self-worth. A nice guy is a man who does not stand up for himself, what he believes in or what he wants, and will let other people take advantage of him. He is a boy in an adult male body, a people pleaser.

I was an extremely Nice Guy. Based on what I learned, being a Nice Guy doesn't work with women. When Nice Guys are trying to court a woman, they typically do the following:

- They are not direct with their intentions and feelings.

- They are afraid they will say the wrong things, make mistakes, or be vulnerable.

- They are afraid to ask for sex directly.

- They are afraid to hurt a woman's feelings. Because of this, they do not say things when they should say them, and as a result, things tend to build up.

- They will do things they do not want to do just to please a woman.

- They give to women with expectations (usually indirect) and get frustrated and resentful when there is no reciprocity.

- They do not stand up for themselves and for what they want.

- They are too available.

Women have a powerful radar that quickly spots Nice Guys. Many Nice Guys like to buy women things; by nature, women love gifts. They usually accept these gifts with the compromise being that the "nice guy" ends up on the friend zone. The nice guy will then feel devastated and wonder why he is so Nice to her, but she doesn't want him romantically.

1.3: How to Become Your Strongest Self

A woman wants a man who is reliable and confident and who goes for what he wants without fear. To a woman, a Nice Guy is weak and unchallenging. When you meet a woman and begin treating her like a goddess, you're setting yourself up for failure, and if you do that, most women will not find you genuine or attractive enough to date.

As part of becoming your best self, when you meet or start dating the woman of your dreams:

Always Express Your True Feelings and Desires

Make her know early on that you want her. Stop beating around the bush and be honest with your intention from the start. This shift alone is powerful enough to change your dating and relationship life forever.

Some men who want a woman in a romantic fashion go about making that happen in an awkward way that causes the woman to friend-zone the man because he is not clear with his intention.

It is better to be clear early on with your desires so that you can know quickly where she stands and move on if she doesn't reciprocate. By not being honest early, you may end up investing yourself emotionally, which means when she eventually rejects you, walking away will be much tougher and more painful. If you are to fail, fail early and move on to the next available woman.

Be Vulnerable Guys

Vulnerability is power. Don't be afraid to fail. If you want her to send you nudes, ask for it. If you do not like the way she is treating you, tell her. If you want her and desire her, tell her. If you want to make love, tell her. Be vulnerable. To take your relationship to another level, you must become vulnerable.

If You Want Sex, Ask for It

Women want sex, too; some even more than men. If you are with your wife and she does not satisfy you in bed, tell her. Make her know you want it. Nice Guys turn to be afraid to ask for this and waiting for the woman to make a move, which in most cases never happens. A woman wants you to take the lead. You are the man.

Don't Be Too Eager to Please Her

If you do not like the way a woman is treating you, tell her but do so in a respectful manner. Tell her even if you think she will not like hearing it. Don't allow things to build up. If you just keep tolerating her mistreatment of you, she will continue doing so. This is part of standing up for yourself. I have done this to a few women, and it made me gain even more of their trust and respect.

If a woman cannot respect you, she cannot love you romantically. A woman will not see you as her rock or feel safe with you if you cannot stand up to her. If she is treating you like a 'young boy' and you're just taking it, she will not trust you, and if she doesn't trust you, it becomes difficult for her to open up to you romantically. Sadly enough, this is where most Nice Guys fail with women. When women test their strength, they fail, and the women end up disappointed.

Let me give you an example of an incident in my life. There once was a woman I was into, and she knew I was attracted to her. One day, she sent me a text message saying I should come to her office to assist her with some printing work. Being clueless, I immediately left my office to meet and help her. When I went into her office, she said, "You came quickly."

Even though I thought I was nice to her by quickly offering my assistance, she saw it differently. She felt like she was controlling me or as if I was too eager to please. Do you know what? I didn't have any success with that woman. There were other instances where I failed "her tests" too. **All women test.**

Don't Be a People Pleaser

Be yourself and avoid doing things with the sole intention of pleasing her. Be true to your words and let your actions match your word. That's how you gain respect.

Let's say you want to watch a football match at 2 PM, and your woman tells you, "Baby, please accompany me for shopping at 2 PM" and you abandon your match just to please her by doing what she has asked you to do. Even though she will initially say thank you, this may cause her to doubt your masculine core. Nice Guys wonder why they do everything a woman asks and are always available for her, yet she is falling in love with some guy who is not doing any of those things. They become miserable and depressed. The thing is the other guy is coming to her from a place of strength, and this makes him more attractive in her eyes. He is not a "Yes" kind of man.

The takeaway here is that you should do things for a woman because you feel deep down that it's right for you to do it and not because you want to please her. If your masculine instinct tells you do this, do it otherwise don't do it.

Give to a woman because that's who you are and not because you think it will make her like you or make her want to have sex with you. Guys, if you're doing the latter, you're deluding yourself and setting yourself up for pain and failure. *Give without any string attached.* Give genuinely.

Always Stand up for Yourself

If a woman you're courting will not open up to you after expressing your desires and interest, walk away. If she is not reciprocating interest, walk away. Sadly, many men continue 'pursuing' a woman even though she has actionably shown her disinterest. By continuing to pursue, you are opening yourself up for disrespect and will make her reject you even more.

A man who has self-worth, who loves and values himself, and who has self-respect will not chase a woman who doesn't want him. Too much chasing leads to rejection. *I once dated a beautiful woman who told me she was changing her phone number because she had guys chasing after her desperately. She said she would tell some that she is not interested, but they would not listen; they kept coming at her intensely. Some used to contact her all the time. Because of this, she had chosen to change her phone number.*

Don't Be Too Available to Her

Have a life outside your woman or the girl you are courting. The mistake some men make is that when they meet a woman they like, they forget about other important areas of their life, such as hobbies, studies, friends, goals, purpose, etc.

They start spending all their time with the woman. This is not a very productive way to grow a relationship. While spending quality time with your woman is important, don't make her the center of your world or constant attention.

Have an Interesting Life; Do Things That Make You Happy

Don't wait for a woman to come into your life for you to be happy. Create your own happiness. Some men think if they have the woman of their dreams, they will be happy. If you think that, you're deluding yourself.

Many people are in relationships but at the same time, miserable. No woman can bring you bliss. Be happy first. Be happy single. A happy person is attractive and true happiness comes from within.

Embrace Daily Self-Growth

Continue growing mentally, physically, spiritually, and financially. Grow daily. Never allow yourself to get to a point in your life where you are no longer growing.

If you apply the points above in your daily life, you will become your best self. I challenge you to put in the work, to work on yourself and master this area of life. Becoming your strongest and best self will help you in other areas of life as well.

Let us now learn how to master the art of attraction in the following chapter:

Chapter 2: Master the Art of Attraction

The evolutionary theory of human attraction states that we choose romantic partners depending on our assessment of 'mate value,' the romantic desirableness of a person based on status and physical appearance.

What this means for you is that your 'mate valuableness' depends mainly on your possession of desirable or attracting traits, qualities, or habits. Mate value can depend on physical attractiveness, resources and status, intelligence, and other such characteristics that increase your desirability and attractiveness depending on the kind of woman you want to attract.

2.1: Whom Do You Want To Attract?

Sit back and ask yourself, "What kind of woman do I want to spend the rest of my life with?" Clarity is power.

When I was struggling with women, my goal was to get a woman or any woman. When I worked on myself and improved my life, women started coming to me in droves, which helped me realize that my previous failures were because I had not been clear about what type of woman I wanted and considered an ideal woman.

Similarly, I have seen men dating for the sake of it without being specific with what they want. By not being specific, so many men have watched as women who could be potential soul mates walk away. The secret to attracting the woman of your dreams and creating a fulfilling relationship begins with first knowing what you want.

Describe the qualities you want in your dream woman

Create a list of the qualities you want in your ideal woman. Don't limit yourself here. Write down ten qualities you desire and number them in order of importance to you.

As an example of the direction you should take, here is a list of qualities I seek in an ideal woman:

Someone honest: I value honesty above everything; this is why honesty is the first item on my list of qualities I seek in a potential mate. No matter how gorgeous a woman looks, if she is dishonest, the dishonesty is a complete turn-off.

Someone respectful: I can't love a woman who doesn't respect me no matter how beautiful she may be. I love it when a woman looks at me with admiration and is well mannered in the way she talks to me, especially amidst a misunderstanding.

By looking at how women talk to their men, it becomes easier to know, which woman holds her man in high esteem (regard) and which one does not. I want a woman who treats people respectfully and you should too.

A giver: It gives me joy when a woman thinks outside the box and gives to her man without the man needing to ask. When I am with a woman who takes and takes without giving as good as she gets, it turns me off. I love someone who is a giver. I believe that true love is a love of giving, not a love of receiving. When a woman thinks that her beauty is everything and that she has nothing else to offer in the relationship, it turns me off.

An excellent communicator: Communication is critical to the success of a relationship. If a woman is not willing to open up to me and have honest conversations, it turns me off.

When a couple fails to communicate, issues build up. I love women who express their true feelings and say what bothers them. I once dated a girl, and things started to get bad and it was real hard work to get her to talk. By her actions, you could tell something was wrong, but she was not just willing to talk so we can resolve issues.

Someone open-minded: I am a very open-minded person who is always open to learning and experiencing new things.

When I come across new ideas, I open up and willingly consider them seriously. This is one of the reasons why I have grown a lot in my life, which is why I want to attract into my life an open-minded woman.

A kind person: I find a kind woman very attractive. I love it when a woman is affectionate, gentle, forgiving, considerate, and generous.

A caring person: I love a woman who is compassionate towards others. A woman who is willing to give to the poor and care for the suffering is in tune with her feminine, nurturing nature and is therefore very endearing and attractive. I want a woman who is willing to contribute to charities and is thoughtful of others.

Someone ambitious, passionate, and supportive: I want a woman who supports my mission in life and is encouraging; a woman who can add value to my life. Value, in this case, includes support, positive emotions, positive energy, admiration, and companionship.

Someone younger than me: I am much more attracted to younger women. At least 5, 6, or more years younger than me.

Someone gorgeous: Over the years, I have done a lot of work on myself, such as better dressing and grooming, improved physique, better financial life, etc. Therefore, I would also want a woman who takes care of herself, someone who does not neglect her physical or emotional wellbeing.

Someone easygoing: My life is drama free. I don't want someone who gets angry at the slightest provocation or who is unwilling to work on fixing relationship issues as they arise. I want an understanding, patient, and forgiving woman.

Once you write down the qualities you want in your dream woman, place this list somewhere visible to you every day. The idea here is to focus on what you want because according to various universal laws such as the law of attraction, you attract into your life that which you focus on most.

Don't just write your list and throw it away. Focus on it daily so that you can build clarity in your mind. Next, write a love letter to this person you have not met yet. As you script this letter, visualize being completely in love with this person. In this letter, tell her everything you adore about her. Write the letter as though you are writing it to someone who is head over heels in love with you as well. The goal here is to see yourself attracting your ideal woman even before it happens. Put your mind to work now by doing this exercise. Become vulnerable now and write down your heart's desire.

2.2: Become the Person You Want to Attract

After your list of qualities and a love letter to your ideal woman, be honest with yourself about whether you possess the traits you want to attract because in life, "like attracts like."

It's unrealistic for a dirty, purposeless man who does not take care of himself to want or desire a driven and ambitious woman who takes care of herself. Some dishonest men say they want an honest woman. Some men poor at communication want a woman who is an excellent communicator. The truth is that if a woman is attractive, confident, and dedicated to personal growth and caring for herself, her attraction will be to a man who does the same.

Henceforth, your goal should be to become the person you want to attract. Be the person on your list. If you notice a lacking quality in your personality, work on adopting it and in so doing, becoming your best self.

For example, if an item on your list of qualities says you want a well-groomed woman that takes care of herself, but you are dirty and care very little about your appearance, start working on this by embarking on personal growth—start taking better care of yourself and your outer appearance. If you want a caring woman who is also a giver but you're selfish, you can work on this by embarking on the journey to being a giver.

Look at your list, see what you lack, and begin working on bettering yourself. Attracting your dream woman into your life starts with you.

Have you ever seen a couple and wondered to yourself, *"Wow, these two look great together, as if they were meant for each other"* or *"have you ever come across couples who are so similar and share the same values?"*

If you have, here is an important thing to remember: such relationships are not happenstances. When you study these couples, you will realize that their shared qualities are what attracted them to each other in the first place.

If you start dating without first becoming clear about what you want and without having a clear idea of the kind of woman you want to attract and date, attracting the right woman into your life is going to prove difficult. Sadly, many men never clarify their desires, which is perhaps why modern society is full of couples with misaligned values and many in very unhappy and even unhealthy relationships.

Most people have goals for business, career, health, finance, etc. but very few take the time to set relationship goals, which makes no sense because relationships are a crucial area of life.

The decision about which woman you choose to spend the rest of your life with is an important one that has the potential to bring you pain or pleasure. Sadly, because of societal pressure, many men rush this decision or make it out of fear. It is common to hear men say, *"Hey, all my friends are getting married. I should get married too."* Some men settle with a woman they know they do not want because they are afraid to end it or because of the belief that age is catching up on them. **Never choose a life partner out of fear**.

On becoming the person you want to attract, the following quote by Neil Strauss encapsulates the underlying message I want to pass: *"Perhaps the biggest mistake I made in the past was that I believed love was about finding the right person. In reality, love is about becoming the right person. Don't look for the person you want to spend your life with. Become the person you want to spend your life with."*

To become a person you want to spend your life with, start investing in yourself today. When you do this, the right woman will gravitate towards you. Men who apply this principle end up in passionate, loving, effortless, and deep, mutually satisfying relationships. Such men are part of the kind of couple people see and say things like, "these two have a great relationship." If you want effortless attraction and a beautiful and meaningful relationship, apply the above.

2.3: Detach From Wanting Someone in Your Life

Desperation and neediness kill attraction. Being desperate and needy is a big turn off. If you want her to reject you, become needy. Don't obsess over the idea of having a girlfriend or wife in your life. Give up the attachment. Attachment to being in a relationship prevents you from being able to attract the woman of your dreams. When you firmly attach yourself to the idea of being with someone or in a relationship, you become less attractive.

A common misconception in modern day society is that to be happy, men need women or to be married. Nothing can be further from the truth. If your goal is to attract a woman who will come and make you happy, you're deluding yourself. Be happy first. If you're miserable and expecting a woman to bring you out of your misery, you will be miserable forever. No woman wants to fix a man. You are responsible for your happiness.

Know what you want in an ideal partner (the process above), but continue to live your best life as a single man. Keep enjoying your life and building fun memories. Engage in your hobbies and live a purposeful life.

I had a friend who was very good with women. What I noticed with him was that his approach to dating was cavalier and unattached. He never focused on dating just one woman; instead, he focused on dating various women regularly. The more he dated one woman after another, the more women seemed to want him. After wondering why this was the case for a short while, it dawned on me that it was because he was coming from a place of abundance.

Women like a man who has options with other women. The trick is not to be too obvious with it. To her, you having options indicate you're a great catch. This has been true in my life. I once dated a woman who showed no initial interest in me but the moment she saw me talking to or walking with other women—some were just friends—her attraction for me increased, and she started calling and texting me.

As a single man, talk and meet more women regularly. Only focus on one woman when she becomes your "girlfriend" or when you both fall in love with each other.

The purpose of meeting as many women as you can is so that you can practice your conversational and interactive skills. This way, when you finally meet and decide to talk to the woman of your dreams, the conversation will flow naturally, and you will come off as confident and therefore attractive. Women like it when a man is confident. *Most women will reject you if they feel you lack confidence or are easy to intimidate.*

Nothing says, "I am a confident man" more than being purposeful and passionate about something. The next chapter discusses the role and value of purpose in attracting the woman of your dreams into your life and establishing a fulfilling relationship.

2.4: Simple Strategies That'll Help You Become A More Attractive Man

Implement the following strategies

Work on your body

This book is an attraction guide, so naturally, having a physically attractive body had to be part of the process.

However, nothing in any of the dating and relationship books, lectures, seminars, course, and videos I've read and attended says having a body like Flex Wheeler's is the ultimate way to attract women or the woman of your dreams.

Working on your body is about diligently working towards physical fitness and less about biceps or abs. As long as you are exercising your body in a way that pushes you outside your comfort zone and leads to overall better health, energy, and confidence, your level of attractiveness will increase.

Be humorous

You will notice humor mentioned several times throughout this book. That's because humor is important to many aspects of dating and relationships. In fact, humor as an attraction factor comes second to confidence. Marilyn Monroe *was right when she said, "If you make a woman laugh, you can make her do anything."*

The laughable thing is that most men try so hard to be witty and humorous but fail miserably. Laughter and joy are natural emotions that no one can fake. Instead of being fake or presenting her with the personality you think she will like, be natural. **Be genuinely interested in her, engage her in light banter, and without a doubt, humor (and joy) will flow naturally**.

A great way to make her laugh and enjoy your company is to use misinterpretation where you take some of her replies and twist them into humorous jibes at her. For instance, take something she says and twist it to make it appear as if she's hitting on you; if you do this well and with a smile on your face, it'll leave her smiling.

Avoid pickup lines

Using pickup lines is a sign of a man that is trying too hard to impress a woman. Please always remember that attractive and confident men do not use pickup lines especially those of the cheesy nature. What these men do is engage women in actual, interesting conversations.

A research study from the State University of New York determined that women respond better to men who use a normal approach, such as "Hello, what's your name?"

Let us now look at the importance of purpose in attracting the woman of your dreams.

Chapter 3: Be Purposeful and Confident

"Don't wait until everything is just right. It will never be perfect. There will always be challenges, obstacles, and less than perfect conditions. So what? Get started now. With each step you take, you will grow stronger and stronger, more and more skilled, more and more self-confident and more and more successful."

Mark Victor Hansen

Don't let a relationship define your identity as a man: lead a purposeful life! So, what is your purpose? Your purpose is your mission in life, your life's work, or the direction in which you intend to steer your life.

Your purpose cannot depend on a particular relationship, especially a romantic relationship with a woman. A man in pursuit of his purpose and that passionately does the things he chooses to pursue is very attractive to a woman.

On the other hand, a man who lacks direction in life, one prone to living each day by chance, is very unattractive: women want a man who is working towards a specific vision.

Answer the following questions as honestly as you can.

- What excites you?

- What wakes you up in the morning and drives you throughout the day?

- What do you want to create?

- What do you enjoy doing?

- What legacy do you want to leave?

- What difference do you want to make?

- What do you like to do?

- What do you want to do or achieve with your life?

- If you could pursue one thing for the rest of your life, what would you choose to pursue?

- Which things or aspects of your existence excite you the most?

If there's a woman you want to attract or if you're currently in a romantic relationship with the woman of your dreams and you choose to spend all your time calling her every hour of the day, she will not appreciate that on a subconscious level. She will wonder whether you lack something to do, which is why you are always on the phone with her. A woman appreciates it more when you spend time doing what you love doing and then later giving her undivided attention and love. If you are spending time with your woman but thinking about some unfinished work you have to complete, she will feel it, and you will both end up dissatisfied.

The importance of having a purpose in life is to make YOU happier, fulfilled, and less needy and reliant on others. When purpose permeates every area of your daily life, you pose no threat to others or show signs of neediness, a reliance on external validation to feel worthy. Neediness is unattractive.

This brings up the following important question. Is there an easy way to determine the things that interest you the most or to discover and define your purpose? The answer is yes; below, you will find tips that should help you in this regard:

3.1: Tips To Help You Define Your Purpose

Your purpose is your reason for being on this planet at this particular time. Implementing the following easy tips should help you define your purpose, which will automatically increase your confidence and masculine energy:

Be a man of action

Contrary to popular belief, you do not think your way into your purpose. You work your way into it. The more you do things that excite you and make you happy, the likelier you are to stumble into your purpose because the more you act, the clearer things become.

When you discover something you like doing, instead of thinking, "Is this my purpose," "will it work out," or "what if I fail," get out of your way and simply run with it.

This will help you stop struggling with finding "the one thing" God created you for—this is a myth BTW; you can be great at many things—and instead place you on the exciting path to growth and discovery. The more you take action, the more explorative you will become, and the clearer your 'destiny' shall become.

Listen to your heart

As men, we often hear that we should listen to our minds more than we listen to our hearts; after all, a man ought to be logic-driven.

However, to discover your passions and purpose, introspect and ask yourself, "Which things do I love?" Naturally, when you discover one or two things that stir your heart, take action because when you feel connected and inspired, you will feel happier and guess what, women find inner happiness very attractive. Moreover, being passionate about something makes you a catch.

Divorce the idea of the "one"

As mentioned earlier, a common misconception is that we all have that "ONE" thing God created us for or to do. Such an approach to living a passionate life will not work, and if you go down that route, you will end up feeling as if something is missing in your life, which will make you a negative and therefore unattractive man. The idea of being "made for just one" thing is very limiting. Divorce yourself from it.

Instead, pursue your passions, and take action towards their fulfillment; make them a daily part of your life. When you start living a passionate life, you start living a purposeful life, which makes you more attractive to women.

3.2: Self-Confidence

Confidence is one of the most attractive character traits. Most women will tell you that compared to good looks, self-confidence, is much, much more attractive.

All the women I've met and interacted with in my life so far have all been vocal about one thing, *"they are attracted to a man's confidence."* I once dated a woman who openly told me that how I asked her out with confidence was why she was unable to resist me.

Men, when you meet a woman whose looks immediately intimidate you, you will not have a chance with her. If you act weak or come across as weak, your chances with her decrease. When she senses weakness, a woman will test a man more. If she feels like she can control you, or that her beauty controls, there will be little to no attraction. A woman will not be intimate with you if she feels superior to you or if you put her on a pedestal. If you work on improving just one quality of your life, please let it be building self-confidence.

Having money, good looks, good career, etc. are just bonuses that make meeting your dream woman a bit easier. A woman can go out with a weak man who has money for safety purposes but will easily cheat on him if she comes across a strong and confident man.

Have you ever wondered why a woman will cheat on a rich man with a man who has nothing in terms of accomplishments? If you have, you probably also wondered what the woman wants or sees in the unaccomplished man. The fundamental thing to note is that the man who has nothing or is broke might have strong self-belief, which makes him very attractive.

If you meet a beautiful woman and as you are talking to her, you act all shaky and nervous, she will reject you. Some may accept you, but most will undoubtedly reject you.

I embarked on personal growth especially in the dating and relationship areas of my life because I came to a point where I had the money, the looks, and was well groomed, but for some reason, the women I liked kept rejecting me. Some were initially attracted to me but would over time want nothing to do with me.

The 'breakups,' if you could even call them that, caused me a lot of emotional pain because none of these women told me why they were rejecting me. My dating and relationship life was devastatingly painful.

My pain pushed me to buy and read many books that promised to help me understand women better. Thanks to the books and blog articles I read, the YouTube videos and online webinars I watched, and the support of some terrific friends, I started understanding why these women were treating me the way they were. I later came to the realization that most of them were rejecting me because I acted weak and unconfident, while others were rejecting me because I "chased" too much, which made me come off needy.

A woman likes it when a man goes after what he wants without fear of rejection. Do not be afraid of rejection. Rejection will not kill you. Women want you to be confident. In fact, every woman desires a man who approaches her confidently, a man who is sure of what he wants and is not afraid to go out and get it even if it means rejection. Women do not want you to put them on a pedestal. If you approach a woman and treat her like a celebrity instead of treating her like a normal human being, she will turn you down. Be natural and confident.

Beautiful women know they are beautiful. If she feels like her beauty is off centering you, she will turn you down. If you believe that because she is so beautiful, you're not deserving of her, she will turn you down.

My goal with this book is to help you become a strong, confident man who is capable of attracting the woman of your dreams into your life. I want to help you internalize the habits and character traits that will help you attract the woman you deserve.

Many men settle for any woman that wants them. That should not be the case. To attract the woman of your dreams, I believe you must work on your shortcomings and pursue your goals in life no matter how challenging the path may become.

Developing your confidence will do more than improve your dating and relationships; it will improve other essential areas of your life as well. What would feel awesome, to be able to walk up to any woman and strike a conversation or to feel powerless or helpless and letting all the women who could be your ideal woman pass you by because you are too afraid to make a move?

Would it not be better to be uncomfortable and embrace the pain right now if doing so means you become a better person, the person you have always wanted to be? How great would your life be if you could easily approach any beautiful woman you like or want without hesitation or mental excuses that talk you out of it? Regret sucks! Be a man of action!

In an earlier chapter, we discussed how beneficial it is to create a list of the qualities you seek in your dream or ideal woman and the value of becoming the person you want to attract. That is not enough. **You also need to start meeting women regularly and visiting the places your ideal woman would likely visit.**

Most women will not approach a man and say, *"Hi! I want you."* Women expect a man to make the first move, which is why increasing your self-confidence is so important. When you're self-confident, approaching attractive women becomes easier and enjoyable. Self-confidence also makes you strong enough to detach from the outcome so that no matter what happens, whether the interaction is positive or negative, your self-esteem does not plummet after a rejection.

If all you do is sit at home watching TV, expecting the woman of your dreams to fall into your lap, you will remain single for a very long time. Take proactive measures to accomplish your goals. If you see her, go for it without hesitation or procrastination. Go for it!

Let me emphasize that confidence is what most women find attractive in a man. When you have this, money, good looks, poise, positive body language, etc. will be bonus points.

3.3: How to Build Masculine Self-Confidence and Energy

To build your self-confidence, practice meeting women every day not just for dating purposes, but also so you can get used to conversing with women and being in their company. Remember, **always treat all women the same**. No matter how beautiful a woman is, never make her feel superior, or as if you don't deserve her. Always believe you have something to offer to a woman in all your encounters.

Appearance is another essential element of masculine self-confidence and energy. Always ensure you are well dressed and groomed. Doing this does not have to cost you an arm and a leg, nor do you have to use fancy facial creams or other "feminine' beauty products.

Have in place an effective grooming process that allows you to appear composed, clean, and organized. Shower, shave, and brush your teeth daily. Dress well before leaving home; with dressing, the rule of thumb is to dress for inner and outward comfort: dress in a way that would not cause you embarrassment if you were to meet a business contact or a woman you would like to date.

Another important thing worth noting, and this is something I have mentioned several times, have goals because a purposeful man is a confident, sexy man. Set goals and do everything in your power to achieve them. Goals are personal promises. When you promise yourself something and actually achieve it, your confidence soars.

For instance, if you say you will talk to one woman today and then actually do it, even if the encounter is not positive, you will feel great and will be more likely to talk to another woman—to put yourself out there. As your confidence and masculine energy increases, set bigger goals that push you outside your comfort zones and towards growth. When you become a person that embraces daily self-growth, you will attract women like moths to a flame.

Chapter 4: Overcome Neediness

As noted in an earlier discussion, neediness and desperation are murderous to attraction. The purpose of this book is to help you attract the woman of your dreams and create a fulfilling relationship.

To help you do this, we need to discuss and understand behaviors that turn women off so that by learning about these behaviors and avoiding them, you can stand out from other men. An attractive woman usually has many men courting her. To win the heart of the woman of your dreams, you must stand out, which you do by being different.

A typical man will meet a beautiful woman, show his interest, and when she gives him her number, he begins calling her 5 times per day, texting her all the time, buying her things, putting her on a pedestal, and giving her nonstop compliments usually without caring whether there is reciprocity or not.

Such a man will then expect the woman to fall in love with him and when it doesn't happen, which it rarely does, he acts surprised and wonders why she dumped him only to go out with a man who does not offer her all the things he does. Women have very powerful neediness radar that no man can hide from.

If you evaluate all your past romantic relationships where a woman dumped you, you will conclude that any of these four factors are why she dumped you:

- Neediness

- Lack of confidence

- Consistently acting weak

- Being too serious and wanting her to commit to a relationship

All the women I have been needy with dumped me with some going as far as wanting nothing to do with me ever again. Most women do not really care about whether you are a good man who has done nice things for her. If a beautiful woman senses neediness and a lack of self-confidence, all your kind gestures will mean nothing and any attraction she may have had towards you will plummet. Some women will take too much kindness or niceness as manipulation, and as you know, women rarely trust manipulative people. She will feel like you're giving her things because you want something from her. The chapter on giving gifts discusses this in detail.

We can define being needy as wanting or needing affection, attention, or reassurance, especially to an excessive degree. If you are serious about attracting the woman of your dreams, don't approach her from a place of neediness. Being needy has not worked for any man so far. To attract, court, and win her over, your approach needs to change.

You should want a woman in your life; you should not need her. Wanting versus needing a woman is why you should have a purposeful life: it makes you attractive and exciting. Your purpose should not be the pursuit of a specific woman.

Your desire should be to attract a woman who wants you, not a woman that you have to beg or convince to be with you. You should aim for natural attraction, not based on money, material things, gifts, etc. In my experience, men who cajoled, begged, convinced, or did some other kind of 'needy' thing to get a woman to be with them often end up in unstable or heartbreaking relationships primarily because the attraction was not mutual from the start.

Sometimes women test a man to see if he is needy. There are instances where you will meet a woman who shows interest, seduces you by acting sexually interested in you, only to pull back and act uninterested. When this happens, a needy man will panic and start chasing her even more. At this point, she will rapidly begin to lose interest and even respect for you.

When a woman begins to pull back, and you know you have been treating her well, let her go, she will come back excited because she has found a man who wants her, but does not need her. By doing so, you are doing something different from what most men are doing.

Most men chase a woman more when she pulls back. When you let her go, she will see how different you are from other men, and her interest in you will increase marginally. Women like it when a man can be happy without her. She likes that you have an awesome life without her. Women do not want to be the only reason for your happiness; that is expecting too much from someone.

In addition to the above, implementing the following will also help you avoid appearing needy:

Embrace trust

Where neediness abounds, mistrust abounds too. You get needy because a woman hurt you or because a relationship didn't turn out well or as expected. The fact that a woman hurt you does not mean every woman you meet will hurt you; learn to trust yourself and others but especially when you are meeting new women and interacting with them.

Avoid assuming the worst of people; meet every woman with joy and trust in your heart; it'll help you keep your calm and avoid coming off as needy.

Detach from reassurance

You will hear me mention many times how no man should give a woman the power to define how he feels about himself. Avoid marrying yourself to external reassurance to feel good about yourself. Yes, appreciate the compliments and kind words when they come from her, but do not be reliant on them for your wellbeing. Remember that an attractive man is a strong man who knows his worth. Women don't fall for men who need constant reassurance.

Stop being agreeable

When we—men especially—meet a woman we want to attract into our lives, we tend to want to do things that make us ultra-agreeable with the belief being that by agreeing to what the woman says, she will consider us worthy mates. It rarely works like that.

Again, remember that women like strong men. A strong man is not agreeable. He speaks his mind in a respectful way, and when something does not align with his values, core beliefs, and goals, he does not do it. A man should be able to speak up and stand up for himself. Women find this very attractive.

Chapter 5: Love and Value Yourself

The secret to attracting the woman of your dreams and creating a fulfilling relationship starts with you, and so does the work.

In an earlier chapter, we talked about becoming the person you want to attract or espousing the core characteristics of the woman you want to court or spend your life with; to add to that, to love others genuinely, you must first love yourself. Learn to love and value yourself.

Psalms 139:14 notes, *"I praise you because I am fearfully and wonderfully made."* As this Bible verse notes, you are uniquely important and valuable. Loving yourself and knowing your value increases your self-confidence, self-worth, and generally helps you feel positive. A man who doesn't love himself or believes he is valuable will let the opinion of a woman or people dictate his life.

When I first started approaching and dating beautiful women, the rejections from my first encounters would leave me devastated for days and feeling as if something was wrong with me, and I was undeserving of love. Often, the rejections made me feel as if I was not good enough, and because of this feeling, I would be sad for many days.

Things changed for me when I started to internalize the fact that I am valuable and that I am wonderfully made. I started loving myself and taking care of myself. I accepted my imperfections.

Today, if a woman rejects me, it does not impact or change the way I see myself. I know I am good looking, worthy, and valuable. A woman should not define who you are. Define yourself, love, and value yourself so much that your confidence knows no bounds.

Years later, I realized that my attitude was much better than that of some of the women who were rejecting me and that I had let their opinion or their "no" influence me negatively and make me unnecessarily sad for days on end.

If you can learn to love yourself, you will be much happier and will learn how to give yourself the best physical and emotional care possible. When you are truly in love with yourself and happy, you stop comparing yourself to others and instead find ways to grow, to be more confident, and to stop worrying so much about other peoples' opinion of you.

5.1: Tips to Help You Love and Value Yourself

Applying the following tips will help you practice self-love:

Have fun by yourself: Enjoy your own company. Do something that makes you happy. For example, if you like swimming, go swimming; if you like movies, go to the cinema; if you like dancing, take yourself out dancing.

Travel once a year: Take trips, go to a new country, and interact with new people. Learn about new cultures.

Forgive yourself: The fact that you made mistakes does not mean you should hate yourself. Forget about the past and move on. Dwelling on your mistakes does not serve you. Loving yourself in spite of the mistakes you have made in the past is great for your self-worth and self-growth.

Surprise and challenge yourself: Do things outside your comfort zone and try new things. Enjoy the newness!

Start a journal: Journal every day. Write about things you are grateful for in your life. Focus on the good in your life and document this in your journal.

Give yourself a break: Don't be too hard on yourself. No one is perfect; don't expect yourself to be.

Learn how to love yourself by saying no to others: You can't dedicate your life to pleasing other people. While it's good to be kind and helpful to others, make time to focus on yourself too. Focusing on yourself is important because you can't give what you don't have. Focusing on yourself especially when you are feeling overwhelmed recharges you so you have something to give to those that matter.

Create a list: Write a list of your accomplishments and be happy with what you have accomplished thus far in life. Congratulate yourself. Focusing on your accomplishments makes you feel good about yourself, which helps you distill happiness from what you have accomplished. Dwell on the positives of your life.

Create a vision board: Visualizing your goals is a great way to be excited and motivated about your future. Creating a vision or dream board helps you focus on what you desire and start loving your life and yourself.

Trust yourself and your instincts: You need to trust yourself before you can trust others. Always listen to your gut and trust how you feel.

Take care of yourself: Sleep for 7-9 hours every day, eat well, exercise, and groom yourself. If you have the power, book yourself a massage, pedicure, and manicure.

Watch your favorite movies, watch a comedy movie, meditate, buy yourself some good clothes, spend time with a mentor or listen to someone who inspires you, smile at yourself in the mirror, head to the gym and sweat your stress with a serious workout, or volunteer to help a cause that means something to you. Engage in creative writing, spend some time praying, play a sport, or sign up to learn something new.

Taking care of yourself is good for your social life and great for pent-up frustration or stress. You can do many more things as a way of taking care of yourself. Do what feels great for you.

Chapter 6: Master the Science of Gift Giving

Only buy gifts for women who love you.

If you have been a victim of giving gifts but not ending up with the woman, write this statement on a post-it note, and pin it on your bedroom wall so that it is always on your mind.

The purpose of this book is to help you attract the woman of your dreams naturally. If a woman doesn't love you, don't buy her a gift. When I didn't know better, I would buy gifts for women who had no interest in me thinking that seeing how kind or nice I was would increase their interest in me. I was wrong. It doesn't work that way!

If you just met a beautiful woman and want to have a chance with her, gifts should be off limit until she is head over heels in love with you. Women are very smart and have very powerful radar that detects your genuineness or lack thereof.

To a woman, buying her gifts or giving her money in the early stages of the courtship comes off as a bribe for sex. Most women will resent you for that and even feel as if you don't love her for her. A woman hates it when you give her something just because you want to get into her pants.

I know some men who are successful and kind, and when they meet a woman they like, they want to give her everything. The problem with this is that a woman doesn't see it that way. She will feel like she doesn't deserve it; some women will even feel pressured as if they have to do something for you in return. Things usually go wrong when such a man wants to move further along the courtship ladder, and the woman starts saying, *"you were giving me all that because of this or because of that"* or *"you were giving me all that because you want to have sex with me."*

Gifts are counterproductive to the dating process and as a man, doing it is a demonstration of weakness, and some women will take advantage of that until you come to your senses.

Buying gifts for a woman does not make her fall for you, love you more, or even feel more attracted to you. If you're buying her presents, you are showing her that you do not think you are good enough as a person and that you have to buy her love.

You don't need to buy a woman's love and affection. Just be your true self. Present yourself as a high value man. That's enough. If you start playing games and buying her things, it'll backfire, and she will lose interest in you. **Only buy gifts for**

girls when you know that they love you and deserve it.

Some women will indeed have sex with you because you gave them money or things. However, since you want an ideal woman, not meaningless sex, do not give gifts in the initial stages of the courtship. Wait until she grows attached to you.

When seeking the woman of your dreams, a woman that may one day become the mother of your children, seek a woman that loves the person you are and the person you will become if you continue working on your passions and purpose. Seeking such a woman is how you build a solid and lasting relationship; coincidentally, this happens only when two people feel attracted to each other's qualities instead of money, gifts, presents, things, cars, etc.

Finally, believe you are good enough and that the personal qualities you possess are enough to attract any woman you desire. Be sure of yourself and believe that women find you attractive as you are. When you develop this mindset, you will not feel the need to buy things as a way to increase attraction. The women you desire will feel naturally attracted to you.

Use what you have learned in this chapter to update your approach.

Chapter 7: Stop Being a Weak Man

Women are attracted to strength, not weakness. Your masculine strength is what will make a woman want to be in a romantic relationship with you. Every woman wants a strong man or a man who makes her feel protected in the face of trouble, a man who will stand up for, and fight for her.

If a woman feels as if she controls you, or that she can push you around, and you don't do anything to stand up for yourself, it will ruin the attraction. "Bad boys" turn women on because they demonstrate dominant qualities; "Nice guys" are the opposite.

When I was still a super 'nice guy,' one woman I was dating once said, "I don't trust you." Curious, I asked her, "What the heck does that mean? I am always nice and honest with you." I then wondered to myself, "How can this woman that I am doing everything for her say she doesn't trust me?"

When I started investing in learning more about dating and relationships, I discovered why she had said that. I was always available to her, always doing what she wanted me to do, I was indirect in my approach with her, and hesitant with my moves. I often failed to stand up for myself and let her walk all over me.

As a result, she doubted my masculine strength, and as you already know, when a woman doesn't trust you, she cannot romantically love you. Because of my weaknesses, she was always testing me and acting very flakey. The more you act weak, the more a woman will test you and act flakey.

When a woman senses weakness, she will begin to test you more and more; testing a man's strength is an automatic response in every woman. I have seen multiple women similarly test men, which is why it's important to learn this stuff: so you know when a woman is testing you and by knowing and preparing, pass her tests. When you pass her test, she will be more attracted to you but will be disappointed when you fail. Worth nothing here is that the more a woman loves you, the lesser she is likely to test you.

7.1: How Women Test Men

Below are a few examples of some tests women use to determine if a man is emotionally strong, a caretaker

The message test

When you send her a message, and she intentionally takes hours to reply, she is testing to see how you will react. If you overreact, her attraction to you decreases. Sending a follow up message only aggravates the situation and makes her want to test you more.

After sending a woman a message, wait until she replies before you send another message. Some men send a woman a message, and when they fail to get any reply, they start insulting and bashing her. Such reactions will get you nowhere and will only reinforce what she already knows: that turning you down is the right decision for her.

The no-call test

When she says she will call you but fails to do so as promised, she is testing you. Some women do this intentionally to see how you react. If she says she will call, wait until she calls you. If you go out of your way and call her again, you will have failed her test because when you do this, it demonstrates neediness, your neediness. Neediness is unattractive.

The "I can control you" test

When she knows you are busy but asks you to do something for her, she is also testing you.

I remember a day when I was in my office working and the woman I was dating at the time sent me a text message saying she would like me to help her with the photocopy machine. I immediately went to help her. Can you guess what happened? The fact that I quickly came surprised her. When I met her, she said, *"You came quickly."*

Leaving what I was doing and immediately going to help her ruined the attraction she felt towards me. It indicated that she could control me, which is not very masculine.

This is not to say you should not help someone you are dating if she requests for your help, but instead, you must ensure that the request is appropriate. In my case, what was wrong was how she made the request. She sat in her office, which was not far from mine, and sent me a text message that I should help her with the photocopy machine. If I knew the knowledge that I now know, I would have stood my ground and said, *"I would really like to help you but I am busy with work right now. If it is urgent, maybe later, when I finish what I am working on."*

Such a response would have made her more respectful of me, but because I acted as an eager-to-please servant in that instance, her attraction towards me lowered and she even admitted that by saying "you came quickly." Remember, your masculine strength is what will attract and keep the woman of your dreams.

As a man, you must ensure that your woman knows that you will not accept second-class treatment. Ensure she knows that you will not stand for ill treatment from her or from anyone else for that matter. If a woman is walking all over you and you are doing nothing about it, you are failing as a man.

When you get into a situation where a woman you want displays controlling behavior, because you are a strong man, choose to walk away because you know you deserve the best. That will also tell her that you know your worth and that you love and value yourself. When you love yourself, you cannot sit idly by as someone pushes you around as if you are a nobody. If you are treating a woman respectfully and loving her and she is not reciprocating, walk away as quickly as you can and find someone better.

Remember: always demonstrate a masculine vibe. Women find confidence, masculinity, and humor highly attractive. Masculine energy is all about drive, purpose, mission, and achieving goals, breaking through barriers, etc. It is also direct, decisive, and fearless. Women like men who pursue what they want in spite of their fears and potential for failure.

Even when she rejects you, a woman will respect you more when you fearlessly go for a kiss on a date, or you quickly get to the point and try to set a date when you meet her for the first time.

Being successful in any endeavor in life requires a commitment so strong that it remains undeterred by failure or rejection. Dating is similar; look at it as a process of getting through the No's to get to the Yeses.

Chapter 8: Understand that Women Want Sex Too

Sex is an essential part of any romantic relationship. Many scientific studies have concluded that sex helps strengthen the relational bond existing between lovers, and cements a broader sense of intimacy in a loving relationship. Whether you are in a long-term relationship or starting a new one, do not overlook the importance of sex to your overall emotional wellbeing. Sex also plays a crucial role in maintaining a healthy relationship.

Women want sex just as much as men do, if not more. The difference is that women have more self-control and need to feel safe, comfortable, and secure with a man before having sex with him whereas if given a chance to be sexually intimate with a beautiful woman, most men would have sex with her right away.

From a woman's perspective, sex has many implications such as pregnancy, emotional abuse, infections, etc., which is why it makes sense that before having sex with you, a woman will first evaluate you as a potential suitor and make sure you pass her tests.

In addition to that, most women want the man to make the first move. Very few women are comfortable enough to walk up to a man and say, *"Hey! I want to have sex with you."*

Some men allow fear to control them so much that they get into a relationship with a woman for so long without ever making the 'sex move' thinking that it might offend the woman or something. Such a man is likely to take the woman on various dates and spend money on her, and even when the woman shows signs of wanting him sexually, he never makes his move because he is too afraid of rejection.

When a woman loves you, she will want to have sex with you. If you hesitate and fail to make 'the move,' her interest in you gradually starts to wane. Some women will assume you are weak, timid, or lacking confidence, and others will assume you don't find them sexually desirable.

Many 'nice guys' have intimacy problems, which is why they hesitate a lot and never make a move. When I was a 'nice guy,' I used to hesitate because I thought making a move might offend the woman I was dating. Guess what, some women who were initially interested in me gradually lost interest. It is better to make a move and let her say no than not make it at all.

If you ever want to get intimate with a woman or have sex with her, you must be willing to be vulnerable and express your desire. As mentioned earlier, women have a lot of self-control regarding sex. If you don't make a move, she will just keep going out with you and eventually do it with a man who has the guts to make a move.

When you hesitate a lot, especially when she is highly attracted to you, she will wonder what kind of man you are. Women want sex too. Most women will sleep with a man after the third date especially if he has treated her well and made her feel safe and comfortable with him, but for that to happen, the man has to lead her.

It is important to mention again that the purpose of this book is to help you attract the woman of your dreams and create a fulfilling relationship. To achieve this goal, you need to focus beyond sex. Most women will not appreciate it if all you care about is having sex with her. If you want to build a stable relationship, you have to look beyond sex.

An earlier chapter talked about creating a list of the qualities you want in your dream woman. These qualities are what you should be looking out for when dating so you can find the right match for you. These qualities are what will make you desire to be with a woman after you've had sex with her. I can't stress this enough. I have seen many men focus on sex as if it the most critical thing in a relationship, which it's not.

A woman once told me that if you ever want your woman to respect you, make her know that her vagina doesn't control you. She said she considers some men grown-up kids because of the high value they place on her vagina so much so that they give away all their power, which then makes her feel superior to these men. Because she felt superior, she would not have sex with such men.

No strong and confident men would ever let sex control him. **Don't put a woman on a pedestal**. Your focus should always be on courting your woman correctly, making her laugh, taking her to lovely places on dates, making her feel comfortable, being masculine, confident, etc. When you do this, she will be all too eager and happy to open up to you.

You cannot talk a woman into having sex with you. Never negotiate for sex; you want your woman to want sex and not use it as some advantage. You and your woman should see sex as something that benefits each of you and the relationship. Sex between partners helps maintain an overall sense of wellbeing, which is why when you find the woman of your dreams, have sex regularly; the more you want her, the more desired and valued she'll feel, and the more attached to you she will become

Chapter 9: Know When to Make Your Move

No matter how good looking or wealthy you may be, it is your responsibility as a man to approach a woman. Don't expect a woman to approach you: Man up and make your move.

Many men are single because they are not proactive. Some men focus only on their business, career, school, etc. and complain that they can't find the woman of their dreams. If you don't put yourself out there, how will you find the woman of your dreams?

Women, even those highly interested in you, rarely make the first move; they expect you to be a man and do what a man ought to do: be the first to make a move. If you hesitate when she is showing interest in you, she will assume you lack confidence, and as mentioned earlier, women consider a lack of confidence a big turn off.

Every man should develop the confidence to approach any woman and start a conversation. Many men suffer from approach anxiety. As a result, they never make the first move. How many times have you seen a woman you want passing by but froze?

You must develop your courage and overcome the fear of approaching women. You must overcome the fear of rejection. Even if she turns you down, be happy with yourself that you made a move. The only way to overcome approach anxiety is to do it: put yourself out there. The more you do it, the easier it becomes.

I used to suffer from approach anxiety. My suffering has made me a better person because it made me want to learn more about women and dating. In the past, when I met a woman I liked, I would be nervous and anxious, and because many women could feel and see the nervousness and anxiousness in my energy and body language, they rejected me.

Because of the pain of those experiences, I became even more determined to master this area of my life. In spite of my fear, I decided to be the man making a move, to approach as many women as I could until I got better at it. Out of fear, I would meet many women I liked but was too afraid to make any move because I was stuck in analysis paralysis and fearful thoughts. After such encounters, I would go home feeling like a complete failure. In addition to that, the women who rejected me also made me feel incredibly bad about myself. I was sad and often felt as if something was wrong with me.

My mentality started to change when I saw some of my friends who were excellent and confident with women also getting rejected. What I realized from my friends was that they moved on very quickly and didn't let the rejection determine their self-worth. They were still happy even though they got rejected. They did not allow the rejection to define who they were. The following day, they would be out there talking to new women whereas each time I got rejected, I didn't want to meet a woman again. I would spend months in emotional anguish before getting over it.

As I embarked on self-growth, I started to realize that I was good enough and that a woman rejecting me didn't mean something was wrong with me. This realization became more profound when I realized that rejections are part of life: celebrities get rejected all the time; even Jesus Christ was rejected by many. Knowing this helped me realize that I am not an exception to the rule and that not every woman I met would automatically want to be with me. Some, if not many, would reject me and I would still be OK because rejection is part of life.

Not every woman you meet will accept you. Take comfort in the fact that you approached her. Be happy that you approached her. Today, when a woman rejects me, I leave smiling and joyful for the fact that I made a move and didn't let her walk past me. At least, there is no regret on my part. It is better to try and fail than to not try at all. Never let a woman you like to walk past you. Try, to be proactive; if you fail, you will walk away knowing that you tried.

You need to understand that you grow the most when there is the highest level of fear of failure. Always go where your fear leads you. Whatever you are most afraid of is the very thing you must do to grow. If you have a full-time job and are busy throughout the week, commit to meeting at least two women over the weekend. If you do so, you will meet a woman who likes you just as much as you like her. Meeting many women gives you options and fosters an abundance mindset. It is not possible to be needy when you have many women to choose from versus when you are pursuing one girl who doesn't even want you.

9.1: Where to Meet Women

Since you already know the kind of woman you want (the list you created earlier), and that you must meet women and be proactive about approaching them, the following are places where you can meet women and ask them out:

- Seminars

- Conferences

- Grocery stores

- Nightclubs

- Wedding/Marriage ceremonies

- Bars

- Shopping Malls

- On the Street

- Church

- At work

- Sporting events

- The gym

- Club

- In School

- University campuses

- Restaurants

- Public/Private Swimming pools

- Lounges

- Farmers markets

- Yoga class

- Concerts

- Coffee shops

- Bookstores

- Comedy clubs

- Niche business events

- Niche hobby events

- Beaches

- Art shows

- Private parties

- Trade shows

- Social events

Always be having fun. Go places you love, and do things you love. Your dream woman will be a woman whose interests are mainly similar to yours. Similar interests with a woman make it easier to have meaningful conversations. From the above, you can see that you can meet women just about anywhere. Take action today. Go out and meet as many women as you possibly can.

9.2: How to Approach Women

Your initial interaction with a woman is so critical that if you fail to get it right, it diminishes your chances with her. When your first interaction with a woman is good, dating her will be a lot easier than in an instance where things didn't start well.

When a woman has formed an opinion of you, it will take a lot of work to get her to see you differently. For example, if in your first interaction, she perceived you as lacking confidence, getting her to open up will be difficult. It is sometimes better to move on if the start of your interaction is not great. I learned this the hard way.

On my self-growth dating and relationship journey, I met many women where the first interaction was not good, but because I was so attracted to them, I didn't give up; I kept trying. Honestly, it was an incredible waste of time on my part because the more I tried, the more these women resisted, and the more they tested me.

The women that I have been successful with are those with whom things started well. That's why it's good to make a good first impression. It's better to start well and make mistakes later. When the first impression she has of you is good, she will easily forgive or ignore later mistakes, but if you show

66

weaknesses at the very beginning, it will be close to impossible for her to give you a chance unless she is highly attracted to you.

When a woman has a higher level of attraction for you, your mistakes are tolerable, but if her attraction is low or average, you stand no chance. Walk away and save yourself a lot of wasted time, and so that you can give another woman an opportunity. I am not saying that a poor interaction at the beginning cannot turn into something amazing. It can happen, but such cases are rare and usually require the man to do a lot of work.

I previously mentioned that you should never let a woman you like to pass you by. I said you should boldly make your move and ask her out. You can do this by following the steps below:

#1: Mind your approach

Approach her from the front, not the back. You don't want to scare her. Your goal is to lower her guard.

#2: Smile

Smile at her to soften the situation and to make her feel safe.

#3: Eye contact

Maintain good eye contact.

#4: Confidence

Be confident.

#5: Mind your approach

Ask for her name with a strong vocal tonality. Use the following line *"Hi, what's your name?"* and wait for her response. She may say something along the lines of *"My name is Stephanie."* At this point, do not volunteer your name. Instead, say, *"Well, Stephanie, it is nice to meet you,"* without volunteering your name. What you're trying to do here is read her attraction.

A woman who inquires after your name is usually more attracted to you than a woman who does not. Always be reading a woman's level of attraction. Your goal when you first meet a woman you want is to be able to judge her level of attraction for you. If it appears that she has a high level of attraction, then you want to get her phone number or a way to contact her.

#6: Maintain an air of mystery

Remain mysterious and let her do most of the talking. A mistake men make when they meet a woman is that they talk too much and reveal everything about themselves, which is counterproductive to the attraction process. Don't volunteer information; let her dig it out of you.

Women like mystery. When you say everything about yourself, there is no mystery, and getting her to agree to a date with you will be difficult. I have made such mistakes many times in the past. With these women, I did not get any chance for a date because they already knew everything about me from the first meeting and didn't see why we should meet. There was no excitement.

A woman once told me about how shocking she finds it that men reveal so much about themselves to her without her even asking about. She told me how when men show her too much interest; she takes them for granted.

Today, my dating motto is simple: ***"If she doesn't ask, I will not tell."*** I only provide information to a woman if she asks for it. If she doesn't ask, I withhold the information. I have had tremendous success doing this. When I am more mysterious, it leaves the woman wanting to know more about me. When I have been mysterious with women, my success rate has been higher compared to instances where I went ahead and revealed everything about myself.

Listen, you don't need to prove anything to a woman. Your excellent record, acts of kindness, or the good work you have done means nothing to a woman. She wants to discover herself. If you incessantly talk about how you have done this or that, most women will find it hard to trust you.

I once met a woman I felt instantly attracted to. In the early stages of our interaction, I revealed so much about myself and my accomplishments, thinking it would make her see how great a catch I was. As you can imagine, my revelations had ZERO impact on her level of attraction towards me. In fact, she doubted and distrusted me more.

I want you to remember this: "when you meet a woman you like, let her do most of the talking. It's not about you; it's about her. Talking too much about yourself is a sure way of talking her out of liking you. Unless she is curious enough to ask about you, do not volunteer personal information. Making this simple change will lead to immense success in your dating life.

Another benefit of not volunteering personal information is that you get to see how much attraction she has for you. If a woman never asks anything about you, it means her level of attraction for you is low. With such women, you will have to work extremely hard for a chance at a date. Your goal should be to date women who have shown interest in you. It's fun to date a woman who is interested in you than it is to date a woman who has no or low interest in you.

#7: Be playful and fun

Try to joke with her or tease her. Be playful. If you can make her laugh on the first meet or date, your chances of success are very high. Women like humor. The more you make her laugh, the more positive feelings she will have towards you.

#8: Set a date immediately

If you are confidently sure of her attraction towards you, set a date on the spot. I usually ask something along the lines of "How is your schedule this evening," or "What is your schedule tomorrow?" *"Are you free to get together* or *just simply "are you free"* depending on the time of the day we met. Usually, women tell me whether they are free or not.

Once she acknowledges she is free, you can then say, *"Let's meet up for a drink at XXX place at 7 PM."* Once she agrees to meet at the place and time, give her your phone number, and get hers. This is a good strategy because once she has agreed to go on a date with you, giving you her phone number follows seamlessly because it only makes sense for you to have her number as you have already scheduled a date.

NOTE: If you are not very confident, ask for her phone number so that you can call her to set a date later. Note that the phone is only for setting dates, not getting to know her.

When you call her or text her, the purpose of the text or call should be to set dates. Romantic attraction develops from physical interactions, not from chit chatting on the phone. When you meet a woman physically, you can touch, hug, hold hands, kiss, make eye contact, etc., which doesn't happen on the phone. It's hard to seduce a woman through a communication device. Plan physical dates so that you can be together; that is how her attraction for you will grow.

When you ask for her phone number and she hesitates or says something such as, *"why do you want my number,"* *"give me your number and I will call you instead,"* "I don't have a phone," or "I will give you my number the next time we meet," these are all indicators of her romantic disinterest in you. Very few women will be blunt and say, *"I cannot give you my number because I don't like you that way."* Women usually use indirect means to refuse and hope you can get the hint. If you insist, some women will give you their phone numbers to get rid of you.

I once asked a woman for her phone number, and her reply was, "I will give it to you when we meet again." I asked her, "How sure are you we'll meet again? Having it now makes it easier to get in touch with you." When I insisted, she gave me the number. When I called her later, all my calls went to voice mail. She didn't pick up. When I sent text messages, she never replied. Giving me her number was a way of getting rid of me.

The mistake most men make is that when they meet a woman who behaves in such a manner, they keep insisting and chasing her, not knowing that they are only wasting their time. I made that mistake myself.

Pursuing a woman who is not interested in you doesn't suddenly make her interested in you. When you pursue her after she has shown her disinterest, it will only cause her to run away from you even further and faster. A woman who will give you her phone number without any resistance is a high prospect and one you should consider inviting for a date. You should only be setting dates with women who have shown interest in you.

#9: For dates set over the phone

If she gave you her number, but you didn't set a date on the spot, wait three days before calling her to set a date. After getting a woman's phone number, most men call her immediately, and some even start blowing up her phone by calling her several times a day. Doing this kills anticipation and is a very predictable move that diminishes mystery.

Let's say you met her on Saturday and she gave you her number. Call her on Wednesday or Thursday the following week to set a definite date on Saturday. A definite date means scheduling a specific day, time, and place where you will meet. Don't leave things to chance. For example, don't say, *"Let's meet on Saturday"* or *"Let's meet on Saturday at Thomas Bar."* Instead, say, *"Let's meet on Saturday at Thomas Bar at 7 PM."* The latter is specific and is a better way of setting dates that she will accept. Women like direct men. Another benefit of waiting a couple of days before calling her is that the woman might be the one to call you first, at which point you can just set a date. A woman reaching out to you first is an ideal situation that allows you to focus on setting dates.

When a woman reaches out to you, it usually means she wants you in some way. When she reaches out, your role is to facilitate getting together. Whenever a woman reaches out to me, I assume she wants to see me; I set a date and immediately get off the phone.

When the woman is the first to reach out to you, and you set a date, 99% of the time, she will accept. Most women will not reach out and say, *"I like you so much, and I want to see you. Let's meet."* They will usually call and say, *"How was your day?"* *"I just wanted to hear your voice"* or *"Hey, I'm just calling to see what you're doing."*

All of these are invitations for you to make a way to get together. She is calling to confirm that you love and care about her. If she reaches out to you and you don't make a way to get together, she will assume you don't care for her or want her. She is right to think that. When a woman reaches out to me, and I don't set a date, it's usually because I am not interested. When I am interested in a woman, I always facilitate getting together.

When you approach a woman, always be yourself. Don't try to impress her or begin to think about which pickup lines you will use. Always be simple and natural.

Now that you have set a date, the next step is to make sure that the date goes well enough to warrant another. The next chapter talks about this:

Chapter 10: Ace the First Date

You do not have to take a woman to an expensive restaurant on the first date. The first date is like a foundation upon which your entire courtship shall lay. Your first date is a chance to get to know more about her and to see whether she is your ideal woman. Keep things as simple as possible.

I once invited a woman to a date and took her to an expensive restaurant for dinner. As the evening progressed, I noticed that I was doing all the talking. It was such a boring evening that I felt like I wasted my time (and money) inviting her over.

She had no interest in me; her primary interest was her phone, not me, her dinner companion. As you can see from my case, I took her to an expensive restaurant and spent money but had a very awkward evening. After the date, I didn't ask her out again, and that was also the last time I heard from her.

Just because a woman has accepted go out with you on a first date doesn't mean she will want to be with you or you will want to be with her. On your first date, you may discover that you dislike her personality and she may dislike something about you. Don't be extravagant on your first date.

10.1: Where to Take Her on the First Date

You can take her to the following places for your first date—an ideal place will be somewhere she has never been to before:

- A nice coffee shop

- A good restaurant

- Bowling

- A nice park

- An art museum

- A bar (or outdoor bars)

You want to go somewhere that facilitates conversation, laughing, and having fun together. Don't take her to a cinema or movies on your first date. Going to movies and loud music venues is not a good idea. Talking creates rapport and intimacy. For your first date, only take her to a place where you can talk so you can learn as much as possible about her. All the other fun things can come later. Imagine you are dating five girls and you have to take each one to expensive venues, the dollars add up quickly.

Be a gentleman

It's essential to be on time for your date and to hold the door open for her. Open the car door for her also. When you pick her up or meet her, you are gentleman, not a doormat: be a gentleman!

When you meet her, give her a sincere compliment. Tell her she is beautiful. Remember she has taken time to dress up for you. Compliment her BUT don't overdo it. I typically compliment a woman when I pick her up, and that's it. Don't go overboard with compliments; otherwise, it will come across as inauthentic or as a bribe for sex.

In our previous discussions, I mentioned that if a woman starts forming a negative opinion of you at this early stage, dating her will be very tough and will require tons of work on your part. I made such silly compliments-mistakes in the past.

I remember video chatting with a woman and telling her she is stunning, and she said thanks. Later on in our conversation, I said, *"wow, you're so gorgeous."* She said, *"Come on! You already told me that."*

Beautiful and physically attractive women, in particular, hate the thought of a man being only interested in her for her looks—just as most successful men hate it when a woman is only interested in his money. I have seen this with many beautiful women. If she feels like, "this man only likes me because of my looks," she will reject you. Be very careful with how you use compliments.

Don't overcomplicate things

We—men in general—normally overcomplicate the dating process. The process is relatively simple really: just be your best self or yourself, take minimal action, and let things happen naturally. The best relationship you can have with a woman is a naturally flowing one, a relationship where she loves you for who you are, and you love her for who she is.

On your first date, don't pretend to be someone you are not. Don't begin with lies because one way or another, it will backfire on you. If you are looking to build a solid and healthy relationship, build it on a solid foundation. Plenty of women out there can bring immense joy to your life. There is a saying, *"behind every great man is a great woman."* While there is nothing wrong with being single, I have found that having a good woman in your life can lead to massive self-growth.

Women are very good at seeing some of your blind spot as a man. A good woman can encourage you and push you to bring out the best in you. When you have a good woman by your side, she will want the best for you. I have had friends who were not taking care of themselves and not well groomed, but as soon as they had a girlfriend, I started seeing visible changes. Most started keeping their homes clean and dressing well. I have even seen some men start managing their finances properly, and others became more serious with their business and career.

Keep the conversation light and positive

Another essential thing to remember for your first date is to keep the conversation positive, light, and to avoid serious or negative topics. Joke, banter, and tease her in a playful, non-offensive manner. When women go out, they want to have fun and relax. Ensure her first date with you is a good time.

Since you will be leading the conversation, make it a point to avoid negative topics. Don't start telling her of all the sufferings or hardships you are going through. Making her feel sorry for you does not aid attraction. Besides, the challenges you are facing in your life should be something you discuss with your male friends, not with a woman you just met and that too on a first date.

Women find masculine strength very appealing. A woman wants a strong man. That's why when you go out with a woman, she will want you to take the lead. She will want you to be the one to tell her where to meet, where to take her, etc.

In fact, most women want to be submissive to a man, but the sad thing is that most men are failing in their masculine role.

When you ask a woman, *"where should we meet?"* she is likely to say, *"you tell me where, and I will come?"* That reply is her way of telling you, *"Hey! Take the lead."*

Women enjoy being submissive to a strong and centered man. A woman is usually proud to say to her friends, *"Hey, look! This is my man."* When a woman senses your strength and masculine energy, she will automatically be in her feminine element. Feminine energy is about opening up to receive love, bonding, connection, etc.

Physically, emotionally, mentally, and spiritually, a woman's design is to receive a man. All women want to feel loved, appreciated, and cherished. Sometimes a woman will contact you when she has not heard from you for a while just to get the reassurance that you love her. When a woman wears makeup, dresses up well, does her hair, etc., most of the times, she is doing all this to receive appreciation from men. When your wife dresses sexy or puts on a nice outfit, she does all of that for you, hoping that you notice it.

When a woman stops taking care of herself and is overly bitchy, her man is surely failing. Have you ever seen a woman dump a rich man or reject a rich man only to fall in love with a man who has nothing? That is because the financially disadvantaged man understands women and is probably a master at making her feel loved.

On your first date, let the woman do most of the talking. Remember that the first date is not about you; it's about her. When you talk too much, you are likely to talk her out of liking you.

Let her do most of the talking

On your first and consecutive dates, the woman should be doing about 70-80% of the talking. You want to ask questions. Women love it when a man shows sincere interest and endeavors to know all there is to know about her. Sometimes when I end a date with a woman, she will say, *"I don't know anything about you"* or *"you have not said much about yourself."* Being mysterious is actually very important because it usually leaves the woman wanting to see you again, which makes a second date almost certain.

It's good for a woman to be the one digging out information from you. If she is curious about you, it clearly shows her romantic interest in you. Please don't volunteer personal information when you are dating. A man who talks a lot about himself during a date is ruining attraction because to a woman, it says, *"I am sharing this for validation because I am an insecure, needy man."* Sharing too much is approval-seeking behavior. A woman will read it as deflection from who you are as a person and think to herself, "he comes off as needy, insecure, and unsure of himself."

One of my friends is very successful with women. He has told me stories of having sex with women who knew nothing about him. Guys, volunteering, and telling her about all your successes and achievements will not make her want you more. Let her do most of the talking and simply focus on listening and leading the conversation. Find out as much as possible about her. The person asking the questions is usually the one in control of the conversation.

Mindfully handle sex and past relationship conversations

Sometimes a woman will start talking to you about her past relationships or even ask you question about your past relationships. Make sure not to badmouth your ex-girlfriends or partners, and avoid badmouthing her ex-boyfriends or partners. A woman's intuition is very powerful. How you talk and use body language are two things that women are good at reading. The words you use can kill attraction.

Be very mindful of talking about sex on your first date even if she is the one who brings it up. Most women sleep with men on the second or third date unless she is religious, rule-governed, or structured. Some will even sleep with men on the first date.

Women want sex too, but it all depends on how the man carries himself. Most women dislike it when she feels as if all you want from her is sex. When you talk about sex, do so sparingly, and change the subject at the first naturally occurring chance. Most women have had experiences with men who after having sex with her, dumps her and looks for the next girl.

When a woman knows you are genuinely interested in her, are passing all her tests, and are being masculine, sex shall not be a problem. When you don't make sex such a big deal, she will give it to you very easily. When you value her vagina so much that it controls you, you will not get anything, including sex, her love, admiration, or respect.

Take her to multiple places

Another thing you should do on your first date is taking her to multiple places or venues. Doing this gives the experience of multiple dates. For example, you can start the date by taking her to a nice bar, restaurant, coffee shop, or even a nice park. Spend some time there—about 45 minutes to 1 hour–and then go to another nice location that offers something different such as bowling, dart, etc.

Always be the one who ends these dates. You do not need to spend so many hours with her on your first date. Keeping it short will leave her wanting more. When you keep it short and give her a good time, she will be the one asking you about when you will go out again. It's always better when the woman is the one bringing up the idea of meeting and going out. If she is chasing you, she is not dumping you. A woman who is asking to go out with you is interested in you. When she opens the door for you, all you have to do is walk through it.

Sometimes a woman will show a clear interest in a man, but the man will be too blind to see it. The man then continues pursuing her even though she has already shown interest in him. When a woman has shown interest in you, you do not need to pursue her; you simply need to reciprocate. If she suggests you get together or go out on a date, you simply make it happen by scheduling a date and getting off the phone. You do not need to be calling her every day. Your focus should be on setting dates once or twice a week and having a good time together. Once she falls in love with you, she shall want to be by your side all the time.

Escalate things

To ensure you don't end up friend zoned by a woman, escalate things. On your first date, touch her, sit close to her, hold her hands, and make her feel comfortable. When you touch, hug, or hold hands, it lets the woman know you are not scared of her, which makes her more comfortable with you. At the end of your first date, go for a goodnight kiss on the lips. A woman who is interested in you will kiss you back.

If she turns her head and you get her cheek, it shows she doesn't have any romantic interest in you. At this point, you know that going out with her again would be a waste of your time. I typically give a woman a maximum of three dates; if she doesn't open up within this time, I walk away.

You should only be dating or spending time with women who feel highly attracted to you. After giving her a good night kiss, say, *"I had a good time,"* or *"It was a nice evening."* Don't elaborate! Stay in your center and leave her wondering just how good of a time you had.

Make her think about whether everything went all right or not, and replay the date in her mind looking back on all the clues. You are not going to give her the answer. You are going to remain a mystery. The whole time she is thinking about you, and how the date went, her attraction level towards you is increasing.

After the kiss, leave without telling her whether you shall call her, setting up the next date, or even talking about going out again. You are going to leave her wondering. It's a scientific fact that women feel more attracted to men whose feelings are unclear.

Whenever you go on a date with a woman, always have ready a place where you can take her if everything goes well on your date. Remember, a woman who is interested in you romantically will want to have sex with you unless she has some rules she is respecting or is religious. For sex to happen, though, you must initiate it. If you keep hesitating, another man will take your place.

Before going out with her, make sure you have a room where you can spend time together. If you don't have your place, you can book a room at a hotel. Some women will not like the idea of going to a hotel, so it is best to have your personal space where you can take her after the date.

You can also go to her place, but this is risky since some women you date will have "undisclosed boyfriends," which may then lead to all sorts of problems if the boyfriend finds you together. Some men even pay their girlfriend's rent. Can you imagine what would happen if a man who is paying a woman's rent finds her cheating on him with you? Is that not how crimes of passion happen?

Get your expectations right

Finally, don't go into any relationship with the thought of what you can get out of it. You should get into a relationship to give. When your focus is on giving and not on receiving, you will not get hurt. Emotional hurt usually means we have unmet expectations.

Sometimes a woman will reject you, later realize she made a mistake, and come back. This happens very often, especially if you did things right, which means always focusing on making your time with her a fun experience. That is how you need to approach all the relationships and women in your life. Always go into it to have fun, be playful, and be a strong, confident, centered man. If you do this, you will naturally attract the woman of your dreams.

Chapter 11: Let Her Do the Choosing

I say this to all my friends: go for women who choose you. Going after a woman who doesn't want you is a disservice to yourself and her as well.

An older man once told me that whenever a woman rejects you, you should be thankful to God because she is not the one meant for you and that the right one will come and stay.

Some women will usually play hard to get at the beginning, which is why in the previous chapter, I mentioned how I give a woman three dates or chances, at which point if she does not open up, I walk away. In some courtships, the beginning is tough, or the woman plays hard to get, but when she opens up, the relationship ends up magical. Just be flexible in your approach. A woman may be playing hard to get or may not want you to think she is easy, but once she opens up, she falls madly in love with you.

Some women are dealing with emotional pain and hurt from previous relationships such that when they meet the next man, they will test him for sincere interest. If you like her, don't give up the first time you make your move. Try your luck a few times, for me, this number is three, and if there is no change, walk away.

Once you walk away, don't look back; this is very important. The ball is now on her side, and it will be up to her to decide whether she wants you or not. If she comes back, then I know she wants me and has decided to be with me completely.

You cannot beg a woman into being with you. You are a valuable person. You are fearfully and wonderfully made and a unique individual. We have so many women; it makes no sense to remain attached to a woman who doesn't want you. Once you believe you can have an even better woman, you will no longer give a second of your attention to a woman who doesn't see your worth or value as a man.

Never let rejection or a woman diminish you. Be grateful that you approached her and was attracted to her. You were attracted to her; this means you can be attracted to another woman. Be happy with yourself that you took action and approached her. That means you are doing something. With enough practice, you will surely meet a beautiful woman who likes you as much as you like her. You will surely meet a woman who sees you the way you see her.

When a woman chooses you, the experience becomes fantastic because it allows you to focus on your purpose as a man versus worrying about what you could do to make a particular woman want you.

The idea of a relationship, marriage, girlfriend, commitment, etc. should be her idea. She should be the one pushing for a relationship or asking when you are going to get married. All you have to do as a man is focus on dating. When she contacts you, set the next date. Simply focus on having a good time with her. Once she is in love with you, she will want to be with you all the time. She will want to be exclusive with you. It should be up to the woman to want to be in a relationship with you.

What if she does not choose you? How then do you handle rejection?

Chapter 12: Handle Rejection and Jealousy Well

"A rejection is nothing more than a necessary step in the pursuit of success."

Bo Bennett

Never let rejection diminish you or make you feel worthless. When you start taking action and meeting women, rejection will be part of the growth process; hence, there is no escape from this.

Not every woman you meet will like you or respond positively to your approach. Expect and even welcome rejection. The good thing is that among all the Nos, there will be women who will be interested in you. If one woman rejects you, it does not mean you will not find another woman who cherishes and adores you.

As you start taking action to meet women, when one rejects you, it should motivate you to approach more women. The more women reject you; the more rejection stops meaning much to you. As a man, you are not perfect; no one is. The fact that a pretty woman rejects you does not mean something is wrong with you.

I know rejection can be painful, especially when you feel attached to a woman or have feelings for her, but I have learned from experience that things always get better with time. Rejections often cause negative thoughts that try to make you feel unworthy. You must not give in! You should not stop dating just because one woman rejected you. There are plenty of fish in the ocean. When one woman rejects you, move on to the next one, and then the next, and so on until you finally find the woman of your dreams.

Your mindset is an essential part of handling rejection, the right way. View rejection as her giving up a chance to be with the awesome person you are and move on quickly. Your happiness in life should not depend on how women respond to you. You should continue being happy whether she responds favorably or not. View rejection as her loss.

Don't base your success on other people's opinion of you. Your criteria for success should be "Did I take action? Did I express myself? "Am I living according to my values? Am I letting go?"

You cannot make everyone happy. All you can do is be yourself and share who you are and what you value. If it works in your favor, awesome; if it doesn't, move on, such is the nature of life; anytime you are stepping out of your comfort zone, be happy because you are being you, and destroying limiting beliefs and social conditioning that has held you back for years.

Many people lead lives of quiet desperation and never take any risk. The fact that you dared to walk up to her and express your desire should fill you with personal pride. Out of fear, very few men do that. Because you are taking action, say to yourself, *"yes, she has rejected me, but I know I am an awesome, valuable, handsome man."*

It's essential to know who you are. When you know who you are, the opinion or reaction of others stops meaning so much. If someone says you are ugly, you just laugh it off because you know you are handsome. If deep down, you know and believe you are handsome, no matter what someone says to you, it will not negatively influence your confidence or self-esteem. Concentrate more on the actions you're taking and less on her reaction or the outcome. That is how you set yourself free.

Finally, whenever a woman rejects you, avoid thinking that your world is over or that you will never get the woman or wife you want. Such negative thoughts will only make you negative and ruin your life further. Every situation in life is always something you can learn from it. Some disappointments can be blessings in disguise.

Think about it; you have your health, you have your looks, you have a good career, you have your arms and legs, you have your sight, etc., and yet you are letting a rejection consistently beat you down or make you so bitter and sad that these emotions crisscross your face. Always know that some people wish they could be you. If a handicap or a blind person is happy and courageously living his life, why not you?

12.1: How to Handle Jealousy

Jealousy kills relationships and makes you less attractive to women. If you have the habit of feeling jealous, you should consider working on yourself.

Feelings of jealousy come from feeling not good enough to have someone love you for who you are. No relationship where a partner feels this way can be healthy. When you are jealous, you are the problem, not the woman. Jealousy can make you do the stupidest of things in a relationship. I have seen jealousy cause couples to fight over petty things. You cannot be in a happy and fulfilling relationship if you are jealous of your partner.

Jealous men are often controlling, especially when their woman's actions do not meet their expectation. When you try to control the people you love or those that you want to love you, naturally, there will be an impending loss of freedom, which leads to rejection, arguments, drama, and unnecessary problems.

You need to give others the space to choose to be with you or not. If you seek to force their hand, manipulate, or control them into choosing you or staying with you, your fear-based action will make what you fear a reality, and they will leave you to seek someone who gives them the freedom, unconditional love, and the respect they deserve.

Think of a woman as a gorgeous butterfly that lands on your hand. When it's there, you want to cherish and appreciate it. You might want to curl your finger a little bit to protect it from the wind, but when you do so, be careful not to suffocate it.

Do not be jealous and insecure. Do not come up with rules such as *"you can't do this; you can't do that, where were you this weekend, where were you last night, you didn't call me, etc."* If you do that, guess what will happen? You are going to trap the butterfly, it will become resentful and is likely to fly away from you the first chance it gets.

Being jealous and insecure is the worst things any man can do. Jealous and insecure people become overly protective, strict, controlling of their partner, and very domineering. Be okay and comfortable with your butterfly just being there. That butterfly could leave; like a butterfly, your dream woman could leave you. You have to be okay with that. You have to be comfortable with that because when you give your butterfly the freedom to leave, but she chooses to stay, you will know that you have found a woman worth keeping.

Stop fearing that your woman will leave you because you will attract the same result. When you are afraid that a woman you like will leave you, she will eventually leave you. Your fear of her leaving you tells the universe that you don't deserve her, and ultimately, this becomes your reality.

Have confidence in yourself. When you have confidence in who you are, you know your value and your worth, and it does not affect you grievously when other men 'hit on' your beautiful woman because, at the end of the day, you know that she is coming home with/to you. When you have this level of confidence and do not create an uncomfortable environment, your woman will tell you when other men hit on her. That is usually her way of letting you know that she is all yours, she trusts you, and that you can trust her too.

Finally, since jealousy is a fear-based emotion, it's your responsibility to deal with it. If you let it overwhelm you, it will ruin your relationship or any possibility of attracting the woman of your dreams. A gorgeous woman can be initially interested in you, but if she senses you are the jealous type, she will eventually reject you. You have to believe you are good enough for any woman, and that you are worthy of being with her no matter how attractive she may be.

Chapter 13: Be Vulnerable and Stop Taking Things Too Personal

Vulnerability is power; it helps you express your true essence and core. Playing small never serves anybody. You have to be the person the universe meant you to be. Holding onto things and sacrificing who you are to be someone you are not because you think the person you are trying to be is what someone else wants from you makes no one happy.

Your goal should be to be comfortable being yourself and indifferent and unfazed by any test your dream woman throws at you. To be vulnerable is, to be honest, to express your true feelings, and hold nothing back. You cannot be in a romantic relationship with a woman if you do not want to be vulnerable. Expressing your desire for her, letting her know who you really are, and standing up for what you want is being vulnerable.

You may be rejected in the process, your flaws and weaknesses may become bare for her to see, but that is what makes you human: an imperfect being. Demonstrating perfection makes you appear untrustworthy and largely unreal. Give your woman the gift of your heartfelt honesty, and commit to expressing it openly at this moment. Don't let things build up. Never let anything suppress your desire.

Put yourself on the line; put yourself out there for potential rejection. When you are vulnerable, you are expressing who you are inside, and while there is the potential for pain, there is the potential for great pleasure in expressing who you are. You don't want to attract people by being someone you are not; if you do, you will always have to live up to the fake persona, which will cause you an immense amount of pain. Always be vulnerable enough to reveal your true self and stop creating an image that you want others to see, especially in your relationships.

If you're vulnerable and putting your emotions on the table, the people that matter will come forward, and if they don't, then they're not a good fit for you because they're rejecting your authentic self. If you can't be open with your partner, then the relationship is going to fail in the future. If you do it now and she breaks up with you, you're saving yourself years of time and heartache.

Be vulnerable with all the people in your life. Get one hundred percent naked and reveal your true self to the people closest to you and the women in your life.

13.1: Stop Taking Things too Personal

No matter what a woman says or does, do not take it personally or let it affect you. Sometimes women will test to see how strong you are. They will say something to know how you react to it.

If you are always emotional and overly sensitive to what a woman says or does, you are acting more like a woman, and you will struggle in dating and relationships. Do not take what a woman says to you too seriously unless love is flowing deeply and fully at the moment when she says it.

When she says, *"I hate you,"* or *"I don't want to go to the movies,"* it is often more an in-the-moment feeling than a well-considered experience. However, in most cases, since men are not easily moved by feelings and emotions, in most cases, the masculine means what it says.

A man's word is his honor. The feminine says what it feels. A woman's word is her true expression at the moment. It is what she is feeling now. Her feelings, and therefore, what she is going to do, could change in five minutes. It could change every five minutes. I cannot count the number of times some of my female friends and dates have said they would do something only to have a change of mind shortly after.

When I was new to dating, I would get angry when a woman failed to do what she had said she would do. It actually took me a while to realize that "keeping your word" is a masculine trait. When I was starting in dating, I would ask a woman out, and she would say, *"I will call you to confirm."* 99.9% of the time, the women never called back, which left me frustrated and always wondering, *"how come she said she would call but has not done so?"* As my understanding of women grew, I learned to change my perspective.

Today, I do not expect a woman to keep her word. When I ask a woman out on a date, I do not let her call to confirm. I schedule a date or tell her to let me know when she figures out her schedule. Today, it does not bother me as much when a woman does not honor her word. I just laugh at how constantly women change their mind.

One time when I was dating, my plan for the evening was to take her to two separate venues. When we got to the first, she told me how she was not going to go to the second venue and that she has to get back home after our time at the first venue because it was getting late. Can you guess what happened? She accompanied me to the second venue, and we had a good time together.

There were many women that I asked out on a date, and they accepted to come, but when the time of the date came, they ended up not showing up. Angry, I would call and send angry messages or just block her. All that never got me anywhere. With my knowledge today, I just always keep my calm but respectfully let her know that was not the right way to behave.

Most of these women would offer a reasonable explanation, later go out with me, and we would have a grand time.

The point here is no matter what a woman says, no matter how she tries to test you, don't let her think she can get under your skin. Keep it positive. Keep it playful. Don't be offensive or angry; show that you could care less whether she likes you or not. You have to be strong and in your center at all times.

Whenever you fail to obtain from another person something you consider desirable, do not get sad or upset because, in the end, strength and happiness come from within. A woman should not move you because you are a rock, and you know what you are with or without her. Listen to your woman carefully but make your best possible decision from your own deep core. You are a leader!

Chapter 14: Give Her Unconditional Love

Love is patient. Love is kind. It does not envy; it does not boast; it is not proud. It does not dishonor others; it is not self-seeking; it is not easily angered; it keeps no record of wrongs. Love does not delight in evil but rejoices with the truth. It always protects, always trusts, always hopes, and always perseveres.

1 Corinthians 13:4-7 (NIV)

Once you are in a committed relationship and your dream woman is in love with you, give her unconditional love. Below are things you should do to keep the magic alive in your relationship.

NOTE: The following are not things you do with a woman you are courting or one you just started dating.

Accept all her flaws, shortcomings, and faults

No one is perfect, and no relationship is perfect. You cannot stop loving when things go wrong. Love her for who she is. It is amazing to attract a beautiful woman, but her looks should not be all that draws you to her. Looks fade with age, but unconditional love is precisely that: unconditional and not based on any one thing.

Support her (each other) at all times

If you're there when things are good but disappear when the going gets tough, your love for her is conditional. Be there for her when she is sick; if you are not available in her hour of greatest need, what does that make you? You must continue to love her even if health is a challenge.

If you are the type of person who runs away as soon as challenges set in, you are not ready for a committed relationship or marriage. Real love demands that we love through joy, pain, and fear because love conquers all.

Practice forgiveness and reconciliation

Flood your spirit with positive emotions and feelings. Pain is a child of yesterday's sorrows or tomorrow's concerns. There will be times when one of you will do something that will make the other person mad or angry, but you should not let such moments ruin your relationship; grow and learn from them.

Practice selflessness

Do things for her without expecting anything in return. Never negotiate for sex or anything like that. Never say, *"I have done x or y for you, but you're not giving me sex."* Put your lover's needs first; after all, love is about what you give, not what you get.

When you are feeling pain, you are focusing only on yourself. When you feel hurt, focus on the other person, and imagine what she would be feeling. Give to her because that is who you are: a giver who does not care about what comes back in return. If you are feeling pain or thinking, "I'm doing this, I'm doing that for this person," you are focused on what you are getting instead of what you are giving.

You go into a relationship to give. You are not there to focus on what is coming to you in return. Give your woman, your presence, make her laugh, show her a good time, take her out for fun, and do all the little things that make your partner happy.

Always come back together after an argument

It takes two to make a relationship work. Know your lover's soul and know that at her core, she is good. It's probably the reason you are in a relationship with her in the first place.

Help each other grow

Help each other grow and become the best version of yourselves. If you are not growing together, you are growing apart. Help her grow into everything she is capable of becoming as a woman, and she will help you understand and become the type of man you are capable of becoming.

I have seen cases of people who were doing so well in their life enter into a relationship, and suddenly their life starts going downhill. It always pains me when I hear such stories.

Treat her right

Your woman is not your slave; she deserves to be happy. Some men maltreat their woman. She does not deserve that.

Praise her (each other)

Verbally praise her when she does something good. Appreciate each other and even do so publicly.

Trust her (each other)

You cannot build a relationship on a foundation that lacks trust as a key ingredient. Don't share your secrets with other people.

Stand up for her

When others doubt her, be her defender: talk of her amazing qualities.

Take responsibility

When you do something wrong, admit your faults and sincerely apologize. Ego kills relationship. Confidence is healthy; ego is destructive.

Allow yourselves to be vulnerable

When there is unconditional love, there is vulnerability. No one should ever be scared to express his/her true feelings. If you have something to say and it's really bothering you, get if off your chest, but do it in a positive manner. When her guard is up, it means you may not have loved fully or you have been judging her for showing her vulnerable side. When your lover shows you her vulnerable side, she trusts you not to judge them, but rather, to comfort her in her in times of need.

Never hold love back

It's better to love and get hurt than not to love at all.

Love yourself unconditionally

If you love and accept yourself unconditionally, you will love and accept another unconditionally. Complete self-acceptance leads to unconditional love and acceptance of the one you love despite her flaws, shortcomings, and faults.

Bonus: Maintaining Your Relationship

"The purpose of an intimate relationship is to love each other and to help each other grow and become better. Any relationship is about giving and not what you get."

Corey Wayne

Most men know how to attract women, but very few can maintain a relationship. This chapter focuses on the things you should do to keep the magic and passion alive.

Most men become complacent after winning the love of their dream woman. Where I grew up, I had several married women tell me how sweet their husbands were when they were dating and how substantially they have changed since getting married, and that the passion and fun there was at the beginning is no longer part of the relationship.

Here is a secret very few men know: what you do to attract your dream woman until she falls in love with you is what you have to do to keep her. If you don't date your wife or your girlfriend, some other man will. As a man, you have probably wondered how when a woman dumps you or a guy; she is with another man the same week. The truth is that as you were neglecting her and not listening to her, another man was doing the right thing. She had him ready as your replacement.

Women in committed relationships also continue to get approached. I know a beautiful woman who is a 'man magnet: men approach her every day. When at the mall, several men want to talk to her. When at work, a man wants to court her. When walking in the street, men want a chance with her. She told me she would receive about 20 calls per day, all from men wanting to date her. She was the type of woman that will get any man she wanted. She had many options with men.

Imagine being in a relationship with such a woman. When you become complacent and start treating her as if she means nothing because she is already in a relationship with you, do not be surprised if she eventually dumps you for someone better. Courtship is a continual process that lasts until the day you die. It is not a onetime process. Do not say, "Now she is my girlfriend. I don't have to court her or make her happy."

Immediately after doing something that angers your woman, apologize appropriately. Some men let their ego get in the way of offering a sincere apology. Ego ruins relationships. If you are wrong, apologize for it.

After apologizing to her, change the state so she can loosen up and get back into her feminine energy. The best way to do this is with humor. Women love humor. Women find humor and confidence, desirable qualities.

In my dating life, I have not seen a single woman who dislikes humor. Sometimes I will say silly things to a woman, and it will make her laugh intensely. Women tend to love silliness. When she is laughing, she is feeling good, and that is a great way to change her state after you did stuff that pissed her off.

As a man, never dwell on the fact that your woman got mad with you. A woman can be mad with you now, but depending on how you handle the situation, the next minute, she could be telling you about how happy you make her feel. When your woman says she is mad with you, it is how she is feeling at that moment; it's not a firm and determined declaration. Men who don't understand women will take that seriously, and that's how their relationship will begin to fail.

A woman will tell you how she hates you, but come tomorrow; she is the first to proclaim your greatness as a man. Women change their views depending on how they are feeling about the relationship. Never take what she says personally. The best way to judge a woman is through her actions, not what she says.

One time I was out with friends, and one of them got into a fight with his girlfriend to a point where my friend had to abandon her and leave the situation. At the end of the night, I drove her home. Along the way, she kept telling me how she hates him, how immature he is, how she will leave the relationship, etc. Do you know what happened? The following day, they were together holding hands and are still in a relationship to date. All she was saying was how she was feeling at that moment. It didn't necessarily mean action will follow.

The ability to avoid taking things too personally and letting go is a skill you must master if you are to have any success with long-term relationships. Always make sure your relationship has an element of playfulness: do not take things too seriously! After all, the couple that plays together stays together.

Conclusion

I am glad you have read this book until the end. This shows you are strongly committed to improving your dating and relationship life.

My goal with this book is to help you attract the woman of your dreams and create a fulfilling relationship. I firmly believe that when parents are in a happy relationship, it will have a positive effect on children and the world. I did not grow up in a home environment where my parents were in a loving relationship. I had to learn the hard way. I had to invest thousands and thousands of hours into working on myself and overcoming my insecurities.

This book is a collection of everything I have learned about dating and relationships over the years. I have put everything here so that other men can benefit from my experience. This book is my way of paying it forward. My journey began after I went through some painful rejections and breakups. At first, I was mad and thought that something was definitely wrong with me. Today, I have realized that if I did not go through all of that, I would not have the wealth of knowledge that I am now sharing with you.

It is my deepest desire to see happy homes and parents being good examples to their children. I desire that every man who reads this book learns how to take control of his dating and relationship life, and becomes the man that God (or the universe) meant him to be: a great man.

In my experience of life, I have seen many men settle for less than satisfying relationships, get married to the wrong person, or for whatever reasons, settle with a woman they do not love. This book is for men who want more. It is for men who have set a higher standard for themselves and who are committed to attracting the woman of their dreams. It is for men who have been through difficult situations and now want to learn how to take total control of their dating and relationship destiny. I believe you can achieve anything you desire.

Read this book several times and commit to applying the various things you learn from it. Meet women regularly and build your confidence. Be the person you want to attract.

Finally, if this book was helpful, kindly take a moment to write a review on Amazon. I really appreciate all your feedback and would love to hear what you have to say about the book.

Thank you very much for being with me as I shared the various things I have learned about dating, love, and relationship.

Printed in Great Britain
by Amazon

26338492R00071